Aerosols
and Other Poems

Poetry collections and chapbooks by Catharine Savage Brosman

Watering (Athens: University of Georgia Press, 1972)

Abiding Winter (Florence, Ky: R. L. Barth, 1983)

Journeying to Canyon de Chelly (Baton Rouge: LSU Press, 1990)

Passages (Baton Rouge: LSU Press, 1996)

The Swimmer and Other Poems (Edgewood, Ky: R.L. Barth, 2000)

Places in Mind (Baton Rouge: LSU Press, 2000)

Petroglyphs: Poems and Prose (Thibodaux: Jubilee:
A Festival of the Arts, Nicholls State University, 2003)

The Muscled Truce (Baton Rouge: LSU Press, 2003)

Range of Light (Baton Rouge: LSU Press, 2007)

Breakwater (Macon: Mercer University Press, 2009)

Trees in a Park (Thibodaux: Chicory Bloom Press, 2010)

Under the Pergola (Baton Rouge: LSU Press, 2011)

On the North Slope (Macon: Mercer University Press, 2012)

On the Old Plaza (Macon: Mercer University Press, 2014)

A Memory of Manaus (Macon: Mercer University Press, 2017)

Chained Tree, Chained Owls: Quintains
(Columbia: Green Altar / Shotwell Publishing, 2020)

Clara's Bees (UK: Little Gidding Press, 2021)

Arm in Arm (Macon: Mercer University Press, 2022)

Aerosols
and Other Poems

Catharine Savage Brosman

GREEN ALTAR BOOKS
SHOTWELL PUBLISHING

Published by GREEN ALTAR BOOKS, an imprint of
SHOTWELL PUBLISHING LLC

Post Office Box 2592

Columbia, So. Carolina 29202

www.ShotwellPublishing.com

Cover Image: "Doullut House, New Orleans," by Donald Maginnis

ISBN: 978-1-947660-93-9

FIRST EDITION

10 9 8 7 6 5 4 3 2 1

Produced in the Republic of South Carolina

To my daughter, Katherine Brosman Deimling, and her family.

For friends, also, and in memory of the departed whom I loved.

Acknowledgments

Academic Questions: "Anthony and Cleopatra" (translated),
    "Bearings," *"Festschrift,"* "Moon Tracks," "Old Fashioneds,"
    "The Raven Grill";
Alabama Literary Review: "For Jane on Her Ninetieth," "Kale,"
    "Woman with Mop and Bucket";
Arkansas Review: "By the Bywater";
Chronicles: A Magazine of American Culture: "Blue Tarpaulins,"
    "Hit Man";
First Things: "Dinner at Gautreau's," "Dust Bowl";
Moonlight & Magnolias: "Swan Boats."

Photograph credits
All photographs are used by permission.

Cover: "Doullut House," Donald Maginnis;
P. 6, "Blue Heron at Avery Island," Jeannie Wright Miller;
P. 27, "Full Moon and Gray Clouds During Nighttime," Ganapathy
    Kumar, licensed by Unsplash;
P. 46, "Turkey Vultures on a High-Rise Balcony," Carol A. Miller;
P. 51, "Saguaros," Sarah Vesty;
P. 84, "Woman of the High Plains, Texas Panhandle, 1938,"
    Dorothea Lange, Museum of Fine Arts Houston;
P. 109, Author photograph, Lynn Frank.

The author is grateful to the photographers and to Eleanor P. Beebe,
who assisted in the choice of the Lange photograph.

Paul Valéry on Stendhal:

"Il rend ses lecteurs fiers de l'être."
(He makes his readers proud to be so.)

Readers, be proud.

Contents

ELEVEN POEMS ON COCKTAILS

INTRODUCTORY NOTE

THESE POEMS—PUFFS OF AIR, OR "AEROSOLS"—are auras, emanations of being, lingering, prolonging meaning. Following the title poem, they are arranged in sections, structured according to themes, inspirations, forms, or other markers. Among the underlying vectors are perception and imagination—how we see, feel, and picture things. The approach is, loosely, phenomenological. Hence the importance here of painting and of poetry itself. Vision as both tool and matter plays a major role. Vivid scenes, memories, daydreams, and concocted idylls arise from stores of sight, outer and inner. Such visions are essential for personal and collective health.

Motifs, topics, moods, and figures circulate. In the first section, "Fourteen Poems from the Pelican State," landscapes, cityscapes, skyscapes, and additional Louisiana scenes constitute a sort of thematic conversation with one another, then are echoed occasionally later. They are followed by four translations from the French and, in a contrasting mode, "Ten Poems in the Manner of Yüan Hung-tao." "Dancing to the Years" includes poems on memory and time as well as light verse. Next come "Three Arizona Poems," then "Affects," in which various emotions get direct treatment, even as they are part of the fabric of poems there and elsewhere. In "Abroad" readers will find views of various European locations. The organizing conceit of the penultimate section, "A Gallery," is partly ekphrastic, but it illustrates also the reflection of art back on life (in Oscar Wilde's formula, "Life imitates art"). In the final section, "Eleven Poems on Cocktails," despite light-hearted appreciation of individual figures and cordial gatherings, the necessary, universal fate sketched earlier in poems such as "Death Passes" makes its appearance obliquely but more than once.

Here and there, friends as well as family members are featured. Both the quick and the dead are visible. Among the latter is my deceased husband, Patric Savage (1928-2017), "my great companion," a dedicatee of five previous poetry collections of mine. A new figure appears from time to time. Readers will encounter traces of the *coup de foudre* (lightning love) that arose during our shipboard encounter in 2022, a shared "aerosol," spontaneous, ardent, yet platonic.

Aerosols

The whole world goes beyond itself— not just
in bursting stars, but immaterially.
Four random objects on a shelf—they must
mean something, surely! First, of course, to *me*,

here, now, as I too radiate, I trust,
in thoughts, projections, possibility,
regardless of inevitable dust—
well weighted by the import of *to be,*

its heft and grounding. Where would thought expire,
or love? A stone is present fully—dense
idea; emanations of desire

surround us; aerosols hang in suspense—
perfumes of memory, the heart of fire,
an aspen quivering in evidence.

Fourteen Poems from the Pelican State

I

BEARINGS

—New Orleans

No point in saying north, south, east, or west—
you won't be understood. This crescent space
is shaped, sharp-angled, by the river—pressed
from the meridian in its embrace.

We say "downtown" or "uptown," "river," "lake";
concentric avenues contribute sense;
enormous wedges marked out early make
a neat design, providing reference.

An age ago, I lost my bearings—green,
and restless, like my father. Finding true
directions was a long adventure; seen
in retrospect, it's odd at first, askew.

But radii connect, and streets in rows
may narrow, veer, and lead to one I missed;
false parallels converging interpose
a centered nexus. How could I resist?

Blue Tarpaulins

—South Louisiana

Acadia, they call this—not *Arcadia*. Almost. Its towns
string out on both sides of I-10. First, Lake Charles,
where blue tarps from two hurricanes of 2020
advertise the price one pays to live here. At Steamboat Bill's
we get a Cajun lunch. Then Lafayette, Breaux Bridge,
St. Martinville, to study tombs, their frothy stone,
their crumbling names and dates. All beads of memory
to me; exotic to my westerner companions. Tonight,

it's New Iberia. An "Asian-Louisiana seafood" place
seems to be the only eatery—fusion of styles
and races. Next day, we're on old highway 90, east
toward Morgan City, where I found gasoline in the Katrina
exodus. New Orleans is on our minds. But why not
detour a bit, see Thibodaux, Bayou Lafourche,
the cane fields, co-cathedral? In September, though, Ida
blew through, lingered to make sure she'd be remembered,

shredded fields, houses, shacks, and little shops, tonsured
or, like Saint-Denis, decapitated. They're draped now
in blue cowls. We drive the bayou on both sides,
cross bridges, find coffee at PJ's. There is no winning here.
Winds rake over everything; the Gulf devours the land—
the barrier islands, levees, late *chevaux-de-frise*
composed of Christmas trees—the way the north wind
gnaws the moon. Such ruin, in a modest place,

with (mostly) modest folk, the shrimpers, canefield hands,
librarians—rain falling on the just as the unjust.
We set off again, meander, meet le Bayou des Allemands,
Boutté, and cross, on stilts, a cypress swamp
that's turning sick from too much salt. Oh, carry on,
world, carry on, if you must! But, please,
with less extravagance, less wind. Others always pay,
and we are others. Empty music runs among my thoughts.

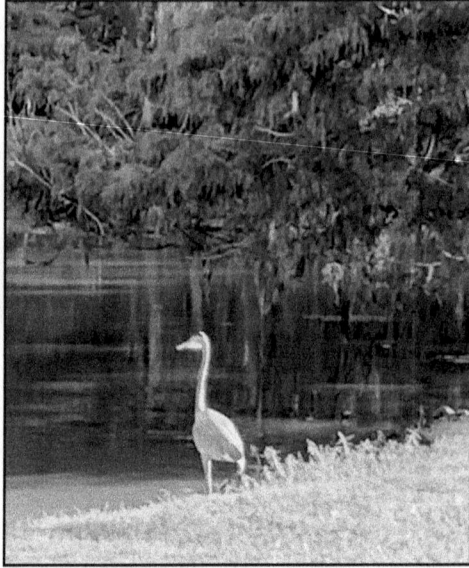

"Blue Heron at Avery Island." By Jeannie Wright Miller.

AVERY ISLAND

It isn't quite an island; it's a salt dome, circumscribed
by wetlands, not the sea. But it's set off, rising, mountain-like,
from the lowland prairies south of New Iberia—a massive
mushroom, with a dense green crest, its trees scraping wispy clouds.
And it's all private, owned by makers
of a pepper sauce. Owned by the past, really, and by birds.
We drive through "Jungle Gardens," nature as it was, mostly,
the way I like it. Here and there, a swampy patch, a bayou,

where the birds are kings: gray-blue herons feathered in perfection,
modeled after Audubon; ospreys; egrets, one on the wing,
others immobile as a still-life. Here's the "Bayou Petite Anse"—
a little cove, a "handle" on the marshy land. A bench invites us, right
at the water's edge. Lovely. But a low-set warning sign
nearby tells us to beware of alligators.
Yes, an ankle, even bony, might be tempting, for it could lead
to better. Precisely: as we consider our response,

one pads his way along a sort of batture, moist, gently inclined—
a handsome specimen of his rough kind, groping
(it would seem) his way to find a sunny spot
for taking in a bit of warmth before the autumn season turns
to chill—maybe getting, too, some extra calories
to last through hibernation. He appears to smile,
almost, his great jaws open, closing slowly, opening again, vaguely
Pavlovian. The foliage around us shakes, not with wind,

but being. In stippled sun and shadow, huge individuals
called pines wave greetings to us; grass
springs back beneath our feet. *How* is the spirit here? I know it *is,*
in all senses—hunger, thirst, sleep, growth,
stretching, mating, waning, dying—and in beauty, God's sure sign
of added pleasure in His industry. Take it, inhabit it,
and add to it your own, your joy, creations, even your suffering,
like that of a lifeless heron, with frantic eye, expiring on the shore.

Scythe

—East Baton Rouge Parish

Tonight the fourth "event" in Louisiana will take place
to publicize my new collection. At the other three,
small, appreciative audiences, in good venues—cozy
bookshops and a mid-sized museum space,
among fine sculpted figures of white bisque and, along
the walls, collages (art's free verse). This time, it's
a lecture room of the main parish library—tables, chairs
in rows, high ceiling, strong light, and a heavy podium,

which separates me, though, from listeners. The director
and an aide are there to see to things—the microphone,
a glass of water, and refreshments at the side.
I arrive early. One man comes in, alone, sits down,
then shortly walks out, not to return. A local devotee
of my art, entering confidently, takes a seat
at the rear. At least she stays. And here comes a critic
(a well-known journalist), carrying prominently

his copy of the book. He too will stay; having praised
the poems in his column, he wants to hear them
in the human voice. That's all—just five, counting me.
Clock hands having moved too far, I must begin.
A sort of seminar, perhaps? I read one poem
pertinent to book-collecting, then leave the podium
and step down to join the critic and director,
hoping (vainly) to herd in also the enthusiast and the aide,

captive, mute. The director and the critic, helpful both,
lead me in a sort of interview. Somehow we make it through.
Offering many thanks to everyone, I leave, not disappointed
but, instead, feeling a sense of purity—as if,
freed of *le vulgaire* and all distractions, one single poem,
rising crystalline in sound, remaining in the ether
of the moment, could be as sharp and beautiful as tonight's
new moon, scything the clouds and reaping nascent stars.

Swan Boats

—New Orleans

—In memory of J. W. C.

A friend and I are out in City Park
by the lagoon. The weather's fine. Beside
the banks, the swan boats beckon, each an ark
for children, lovers, those who want to ride

on wings of avian fantasy, or fate.
My friend tells how her husband, at a curve
along a road in Caddo Parish, late
one evening in a rainstorm, had to swerve

and brake, too fast. A semi-trailer truck
had stalled. His sports car, with its flimsy frame,
was gone, though he walked out. Amazing luck?
Amid the wreckage, someone called his name,

distinctly, adding two short words: *"Not yet."*
It was a deep and otherworldly voice,
both near and distant. He would not forget
it, thanking God and trying to rejoice

in life prolonged, for unsure reasons, less
or great; but still remembering the swan
of darkness hovering, who swoops to press
his mischief on the dance, and then is gone.

DINNER AT GAUTREAU'S

I'm seated at Gautreau's, uptown, with Laine,
fine student, now good friend. Obliged to book
an early hour—few choices in this bane,
the Covid sequel—we take time to look

at wine lists, menus, chatting; appetite's
aroused thereby, and memories. How well
she wrote, with industry and her own lights
enlisted to identify the spell

that poetry can cast from mishap. She,
discrete with men, and proud, yet fell for one
who would not marry her. But destiny
has its own means and will not be undone.

She went to Colorado for the birth,
then gave the child to others. What reward
for all!— their happiness, her proven worth,
his manhood now. We talk it over, shored

together like a seawall, facing force
with force, and mercy for the wounded heart.
The wine arrives, and then a starter course.
It's hard to fathom all these years apart!

A toast to you, Laine—to your steadfast ways,
which let you love an imago unseen—
as those whose past is lost endure, to praise
dim figures wrapped in darkness, strong, serene.

NAPOLEON HOUSE

Ray, Sarah's husband, is in England, his old, native territory,
hiking the South West Coastal Path, counter-clockwise—
Somerset to Devon, Cornwall, into Dorset—
over 600 miles. Alone, thus, she's come here for a meeting
on Canal Street. She'll see to important matters,
then enjoy herself. Having swum and showered
at the Tremé pool, she's walked to meet me at Arnauld's,
at Dauphine and St. Louis Street, for dinner. Afterwards,

we go down to Chartres and its celebrated old-time denizen,
the Napoleon House. Live music and old wood,
of course; photos of the famous; and an ancient bar.
We take seats at the end and order soda water. All manner
of people, of attire are on display, amicably. I muse
on a reception I once held, up narrow stairs, for French literati
(a publisher providing funds). Word of mouth
attracted a long queue of crashers; NOPD men had to flex

their muscles. All because one Anglophobic Nicolas Girod
plotted with Jean Lafitte, after Waterloo, to sail
to St-Helena, snatch the emperor, and bring him here,
this house, this city, ever French in soul, though he had sold
it. Fantasies, mere cobwebs! Or might he have led
a new regime that would restore the fatherland to glory?
More gossamer, my own. Yet an avenue still bears his name,
with drainage sewers underneath and, overhead,

a live oak canopy, a green triumphal arch. Our streets
commemorate his battles: Austerlitz, Marengo, Cadiz, Jena—
plus a general, Desaix, and Elba, isle of exile
and escape. —Sarah's happy; it's not raining here, unlike,
she knows, the coast of England, soaked. She's doubtless glad
the Duke of Wellington prevailed. We pay up, leave,
and take the streetcar home, where we'll relive
the evening, dreams of glory, thoughts of laurel burnt to ash.

II

BY THE BYWATER

We're by the water, certainly, heading for Egania Street,
past Chartres, at the Mississippi levee—way
down river, "back of town," but still New Orleans, near
Holy Cross School, ruined, gone, and Flood Street. We reach
the Industrial Canal, its 1919 steel bascule bridge, and now
the Lower Ninth Ward—but after Katrina, who wants
to use that label? The elevation is three feet; what an invitation
to disaster when the pumps can't empty inundation

after levees break or canals overflow. Oh, Louisiana!—
with your humming bees, thick around sweet olive and hibiscus,
your ripe figs dropping to the ground, bursting,
and their syrupy juice, oozing, feeding the swarming life
around the roots. And your water—lakes, bays, bayous,
hurricanes, river—an artery, or one great suction hose,
drawing liquid value from the upper body of America,
and spreading, once, great alluvial wealth. Is all that meant

to drown us? Not today, at least, a fine fall afternoon.
And now, the street ends, just by what we're looking for—
the Doullut "steamboat houses," almost twins,
from the early 1900s, an idea rolling on the river from St. Louis
with a Japanese design, from the great exhibition honoring
two states. Unique, the blend of styles: dipped roof, deep
eaves, a pilothouse on top, galleries like decks on all four sides,
adorned by looping beads of graduated size, in garlands.

We walk around, admiring, then tour the neighborhood on foot—
"eclectic," with its pastel shotgun houses, singles, doubles,
camelbacks, in rows beside their minuscule side gardens—even
a handsome cottage. Sounds of a guitar and singing,
from a fellow seated on his steps, in full sun, rope us in.
He tells us he was once a lawyer, but retired . . . A ship's horn
sounds. Past and present touch, embrace, moistly,
assume each other's colors, inhabit us—watchers, watched.

ST. PATRICK'S DAY

—The Arts District, New Orleans

All Camp Street sparkles with St. Patrick's cheer—
loud whoops and greetings, bagpipes, sporran, kilt.
At Parasol's today they'll serve green beer
to revelers singing with an Irish lilt.

My nearby errand finished, what it takes
to honor forebears from the Emerald Isle
is see the church of one who chased the snakes
from Eire with unrivaled Celtic style.

A service is in progress. I'm discreet;
I linger in the shadows by the pews,
to listen as the celebrants repeat
in solemn tones of reverence the Good News,

which Patrick bore from England overseas,
to reach the Gaels. He suffered; we do not,
or less. And Christ!—Whose crucifixion frees
us all to flourish in the common lot

of this earth and beyond. The homily,
the sound of bagpipes, organ, human voice,
the shamrock emblems, for the Trinity,
all tell us: love each other, and rejoice.

Louisiana Mountains

—Lake Pontchartrain

There they rise, across the twilit lake, shouldering the sky, thrust
upward from gray water and draped in a pale boa,
with a thought of blue. —Oh, no! They *are* the sky; we're at sea level,
in the lowlands of South Louisiana; they are *clouds*—
as reason tells me nearly right away, but not
before I've been seduced a moment into that old feeling,
when everything has been high plains, of the far horizon breaking
upward from the Llano Estacado and the grasslands of northeast

New Mexico: the thrill of heights divined uncertainly,
materialized in sudden affirmation, by peaks named after Christ's
own blood, still flowing White cowls adorn
them: not Louisiana mist, but snow, snow in June, July. And before
one reaches the high passes, an eery landscape, almost
out of dream, proposes high volcanic cones,
symmetrical, and dark outcroppings of lithic turmoil
erupted from the underworld. All that in my imagination.

Here, rain is falling, darkly, to the south, a curtain lowered
on the left side of the vast proscenium. As clouds rip apart, opening
a pass, the *pièce de résistance* appears, center-stage:
glorious sunlight, silver, gold, trumpeting at us
through lofty sunbeams; and a red medallion dazzles us,
full as a ripe fruit—a discus for the gods of fire. Rejoice
with me: we've got two worlds together; we can gather
time, geologic, sentimental, peaks and valleys, into our pleasure now.

St. Mary Street

—August 31, 2005

No traffic, none at all. Others had departed well before.
Although heading downtown on St. Charles Avenue,
we drove mostly on the uptown lanes, since
a tremendous oak, uprooted, had blown over,
damming the normal route. Eerie. Hopscotching
among many fallen limbs, we turned onto St. Mary,
reached the T-intersection at Carondolet,
and followed it to Calliope. I knew that little trick

to get on the expressway more efficiently—nothing
clever, just eliminating traffic lights. None then;
no electricity. With its steeple like God's index finger,
pointing heavenward, the old brick church
that forms the T meant hope. The broken floodgates
having inundated everything except a slender edge,
a " river sliver," all underpasses filled and one bridge
collapsed, there was no way out on I-10 east

or west, nor I-55 nor across the causeway; only the high
spans above the Mississippi might be reachable,
beyond the swirling waters, then the West Bank roads.
At best, I had a quarter-tank of gasoline. Thank God,
the bridge approaches were entirely clear—no abandoned
cars; we got across. Fuel was not available,
though, since all power was shut off. Following
old US highway 90, we rode on and hoped. More

traffic joined us, fleeing (from where?), merging, going
down to Morgan City for gas or shelter, past
the broad Atchafalaya. Look, an Exxon station!
Though the queue was long, and "Regular" sold out,
no matter. Thus we got to Texas—dry, friendly exile.
Much has been forgotten; but St. Mary Street, the bricks
of First Emmanuel remain, a buoy, a rock in a despairing
land, reminding us that God is with us, always.

AMONG THE MUSES

Just down from my new digs on St. Charles Avenue,
past two saints' streets and gracious old Felicity, still paved
in brick, the Muses start to sing, to dance,
to tell of history and the stars. I follow their procession
as we head downtown. They're not in any order,
and their names, pronounced, are strange, half *à la française*,
half *à l'américaine*, with mongrel sounds
a classicist would not acknowledge. Urania, despite

her cosmic scope, receives short shrift, off-angle,
cramped, and, on one map, anonymous. Years ago,
Calliope—"The Beautifully-Voiced"—became an adjunct,
serving the expressway overhead, the bridge approach.
At least, her name is echoed, as an audio track
starts up when steam pipes from a ship eponymously whistle
their familiar tunes, replaying history
for her, for Clio, similarly shadowy, their own past gone.

Behind us now is she who speaks to me especially, Euterpe,
"The Delightful," muse of lyric poetry, her flute
in hand, wedged between Polymnia and Terpsichore.
Nor is Erato overlooked, she of erotic poetry,
so suited to this steamy place. Melpomene and Thalia
join in—nine genial daughters of Memory
and Zeus, haunters of Parnassus and Hippocrene. It's said
they're jealous of their prowess. Let mere mortals

not compete with them! One does well in life to practice
modesty, discretion—to tread lightly, slip around
gods, oracles, and let them be. No streets here celebrate
the Moirae, goddesses far mightier; the Fates
are everywhere, a-spinning, weighing, measuring, meting
out the thread, watching it fray, finally
snipping it—more forceful than the arts of all
the Muses, any word, song, pantomime they might devise.

Dinner at Clancy's

—*For M. M. B. and in memory of E. W. B.*

It's an uptown place, way uptown, on Annunciation
Street, near Tchoupitoulas, train tracks, levee,
river, port. It's plain, almost anonymous among
old camel-backs, shotgun houses, narrow streets. Too far
for tourists, but known by connoisseurs. Once it was just
a bar; and it still has one, small, intimate.
We're here, my friends and I, to celebrate a sale
we all approve. It is too early yet to claim our table,

so we sit at said delightful bar, where two of us choose
fancy drinks. Waiters pop their heads in through
a Dutch door, calling out their orders, but no one else
is here. Oh, wrong! Together, my two friends
know half of uptown New Orleans and many elsewhere;
one or two walk by. They greet each other;
I get an introduction, and they catch up on Tulane
and De la Salle. Here's someone I know also, back

from teaching days; our brief talk cannot accommodate
all we'd like to say.—Good, the table's ready!
We walk a few feet, to a window. A pleasing note:
as frequently, a group of priests from Holy Name is here;
they know the restaurants uptown. Tonight,
even a monsignor. We are blessed, beyond a doubt:
their sanctity, though off-territory, must have virtue.—
Menu time; how about shrimp rémoulade to start,

then buttery soft-shell crab, creamed spinach? Perfection
in their class! But now I think of pain—a child
lost before he ever lived; two senseless shots
at night, and fourteen surgeries. Pray hard, good pastors,
for your flock and those who've wandered off.
Let's toast the wealth we share in friendship,
in our lives, our work, our great good fortune, often,
and those loves we do not know, God's grace being with us.

FESTSCHRIFT

No need to have a thick *Geburtstag* tome,
or rhyming "Garland" by my writer friends.
My celebration's in New Orleans—home
so long, on which much happiness depends.

I'm seated at a garden party, with my peers,
once students, all accomplished, some retired,
their presence a salute to early years
of molding words and character, shaped, fired.

The spirit was both medium and goal.
Round tables, verbal jousting, tournaments,
with pomp and poetry, the heart of letters,

and scattered wounds, none fatal. You have soul;
you are the champions, the evidence.
I dare one to identify your betters.

Four Translations from the French

José-Maria de Heredia (1842-1905)

ANTHONY AND CLEOPATRA

While Egypt slowly fell asleep below
a sky of smothering heat, the two gazed far
along the river and its fertile scar,
toward the dark delta and the seaward flow.

The Roman felt his heavy breastplate move
when Cleopatra's body, as though part
of his, bent, nearly swooning, on his heart,
triumphant in the strategies of love.

Then, looking upward, practicing surprise—
black tresses and pale countenance, perfume—
she offered him her mouth and her wide eyes,

in which the Emperor saw points of light
on distant waters, cryptic signs, his doom—
a fleet of galleys turning, taking flight.

José-Maria de Heredia

THE CONQUISTADORS

Gyrfalcons taking wing to leave their nest
of carrion, captains, pilots, soldiers, tired
of miserable honor, proud, and fired
by a heroic, brutal dream, sailed west

from Spain, to find the fabled gold
maturing in Cipango. Trade winds bent
their yard-arms toward the unknown Occident,
the distant mines, the fortunes still untold.

Each evening, waiting for an epic day,
men slept, bewitched, in phosphorescent spray,
imagining a glittering mirage,

or watched along the whitened bow and spars,
beneath a foreign sky, a strange montage,
as, from the ocean depths, arose new stars.

Paul Verlaine (1844-1896)

THE SOUND OF THE HORN . . .

The horn's distressed lament disturbs the trees,
a note of pain or sorrow, orphaned, ill,
expiring at the bottom of the hill,
among the nippy barking of the bise.

The wolf's soul, weeping, echoes in this voice,
which rises as the sun starts to decline—
an agony, a coaxing, a dull whine,
dismaying, yet a moment to rejoice.

Contending with the lingering, deadened moan,
the snow is falling in long shafts of lint
across the blood-red setting sun. The tone

resembles an autumnal sigh, a drone,
so low and drowsy is the muffled hint
of mildness where the landscape stretches, lone.

Guillaume Apollinaire (1880-1918)

Hunting Horns

Our history is as noble and tragic
as a tyrant's mask and stance
No melodrama and no magic
no small detail or simple chance
can make this love of ours pathetic

And Thomas de Quincey poor man
drinking opium chaste poison sweet
went dreaming of his hapless Anne
Let us pass let us pass   All is fleet
I shall turn around often as I can

Memories are hunting horns Their span
their sound die out in wind A cheat

Poems in the Manner of Yüan-Hung-tao

"Full Moon and Gray Clouds During Nighttime." By Ganapathy Kumar.

1. MOON TRACKS*

Tonight the moon will glide along its tracks
in cloudless skies. Do I have tracks? And can
I trace them, or, in ignorance, or blind,
presume to follow anyhow? My friend
says, "Let things be," as though our acts

could not be modified. And so I wait,
but then decide I might see better by
the moonlight of my mind than by the sun
and sense. What's shadow may reveal a glow,
and contours of the landscape come alive.

*This poem is from a set of two. The second has not yet been written.

2. THE STONE ITSELF

Yüan-Hung-tao had read for years and years,
and thus he knew a lot. Not satisfied,
it seems, though. Did Yüan-Hung-tao know *things,*
the evanescent rainbow or the stone
itself? This bit of igneous rock contains

a tiny leaf in fossil form, its veining visible.
And here's a piece of wood long petrified,
the ancient grain well marked. I'd like to climb,
as Yüan did, among high trees and crags,
to ask if they remember what they were.

3. RIVER

The river is not far away—at once
a master and a servant, always there.
I hear the whistles and the horns of ships,
and feel the sultry winds that steam with them
from foreign islands. Some day I should take

a paddle-wheeler, see the banks downstream
in strange perspectives, catch the other face—
the batture, levees, wharves—of where I live,
as though to seize the back side of the moon,
new being from new seeing, spectrum, form.

4. Poem on Striving

A bureaucrat of sorts once said to me
he didn't strive. He did his duty, yes;
not more. No challenges—no struggle up
a mountain peak; no mastery of chess,
although his mind was just that sort. And he

was not acquisitive. He had no wish
to imitate the Buddha, understand;
but stress is bad—the heart, the arteries.
Shall I try striving not to strive? So tell
me not to think of poetry and love.

5. Silver Cloud

That silver cloud is moving the wrong way;
or are the others out of line, confused?
The day cannot decide about itself.
Should spring be recognized? Or winter drowse
and loll still? I'll go out, and walk along

the axes of what sunlight there may be.
How wonderful to be alive, and well,
whatever weather may prevail— with friends,
a sunny treasure, making every season good.
Oh, look—a pine tree, sweeping bits of blue!

6. DAWN

Pat looks at me and tries to speak. His eyes
are distant, glazed. He struggles, finds his voice:
"I need for you to take me where I want
to go." I'm willing, certainly. The words
are clear. The meaning? He cannot say more—

a mystery. I press his hand again.
"I'll sing for you." "Juanita" comes to mind,
where southern moonbeams linger, and the dawn
is breaking at the skyline. He will wake
to death tomorrow, loved, in brilliant light.

7. THINGS I'VE SEEN AT CARNIVAL

It's February—Saturnalia,
the dripping fat before the lean of Lent.
The avenue is lively in the dusk,
with milling crowds and pedlars, many dressed
like Harlequins in purple, gold, and green,

some wearing lights on shoes, or fixed in hair,
or sequins on their faces. Everywhere,
long necklaces. The cherry-pickers test
the tree height. Folly and misrule abide—
confined, at least, not rioting, not war.

8. IN THE MOUNTAINS OF WALES

—For W. D. C.

We hike on rocky paths along a stream.
There's no one else. I finally tire. I turn
and leave my younger friend to climb alone.
The rustic inn where we've booked rooms is not
deserted; here's a nosy chap who takes

unholy interest in me. He cannot believe
I'm really with a friend. "And what's his name?"
"He's William Clinton." "Nah!"—the man assumes
it's phoney. So I wait, and watch the fire.
In time, a passport will be passed around.

9. FIRMAMENT

Yüan-Hung-tao looked up at blue, pristine,
and down at clouds. He'd hiked for many miles
to see the sky divide—a doughy mass
below; the azure, an empyreal
ideal. Could he conceive how I can fly

between the layers now on silvery wings
of an enormous dragon? As I drink
my wine, a poem rises here to join
two worlds, two strata, dream recast as words.
Recite for me, Hung-tao, the white, the blue.

10. MOON WALK

—For J. H. C.

It runs along the river front below
the street. I watch two freighters heading down-
stream, with their pilots, toward the bridge. A friend
reminds me that we saw together once
a muffled man in white, and helmeted

transparently, take lightweight, lumbering steps
upon the surface of a distant orb,
announcing through the skies it was for all
mankind. My feet are halfway numb; I don't
walk well on cobblestones. I'll think of him.

Dancing to the Years

THE FULLNESS OF TIME

Thinking ahead in expectation, to a becoming,
carried on by the momentum of the day,
the morrow, one's own tension, concentration,
others' drive, we suppose that all will ripen

in due course, stretching smoothly like a summer
of the past. And that it will be good. Do we want
to count our days, calculate our risks for cancer,
heart disease, bad lungs? Those thunderheads

will soon release the promised rain; their winds
will cool the desert; saplings, little garden plants
that you have tended will mature, and roses
bloom again in autumn. Our hearts will beat

in steady love. Ah, but what we have now *is*
time's fullness. *Was.* What's left is something
else, an empty shoreline, somber skies without
refreshment, letters without reply, all stillborn.

BENDEMEER'S STREAM

I played; Pat sang. Oh, yes.

At a St. Louis school on Arbor Day of '39,
Pat received a potted silver maple tree.
He made a watered place for it in his mother's
garden, by the river bank. His father died
early that year, tubercular, his lungs
devoured by mustard gas at Ypres.

Pat dreamt boys' dreams; later, men's.
Think of what it takes to make a man—
the strange, given being that is self, its drive,
its growing upward on its own,
the frame, the limbs and intellect fulfilled,
all fashioned by the body's law. He kept

in mind the maple—great, green thought.
In 1970 he visited his tree, "magnificent,"
he said—both, however, bearing scars,
his heart a leaky bellows. Ten years
ago, when we returned, we found an absentee,
its shade a cool abstraction. Tom Moore's

old poem lingers with me now, the roses
withered, Pat, too, gone. Distillations
of the past drift by, musty essence,
silvery light at work on leaves—
the stream of our two lives still flowing,
merely underground. Tonight I'll play again.

DEATH PASSES

—in memory of Pat

Death passes in an ambulance, a knell
of modern times. Whose names are on the rolls?
It screams. I think of Donne's immortal bell.
Some will survive; some, DOA. "It tolls

for thee." And I remember those last years,
reduction of the body to a thing
transported, back, then gone again. My tears
are insufficient for the reckoning.

FOR JANE, ON HER NINETIETH

It may be we're not meant for such great age,
enduring past the full "three score and ten."
But there's a time for all things, said a sage,
who, were he here, would see that modern men

call sixty "middle-aged," and ninety, still
in competition. Fifteen years or more
than we, perhaps, is "old"; yet, chance and will
can change horizons outward. With your store

of practice, prudence, your profound belief,
rejoice, sail well the channels that remain,
and let things resonate, the love, the grief.
Congratulations and best wishes, Jane.

Toucan

A lovely carving on my shelf—warm wood,
well wrought, and self-possessed, as though the bird
itself were there. It's beautiful, and good.
Of course—Pat's choice, an image of the Word

in New World avian form. How can inert,
material objects speak? Did Christ not bless
grain, grape, fruit, and perfume—things we convert,
by grace, to life itself and happiness?

The toucan's voice is still, as suits a mind
in meditation. Currents pass, though, caught,
diffuse, implicit for the feathered kind,
who will take wing in motion, meaning, thought.

THE RAVEN GRILL

I
It's not historic—old by just a score
of years—nor otherwise impressive. Still,
it wears its name, poetic, well. The door
invites us by an inkstand, scroll, and quill

to parse its sense. Within, the famous bird
presides in bronze and charcoal, finely drawn,
evoking fleeting days by that one word
it quoth. The past is foreign, always gone,

and *nevermore* to come again. Thank God;
what would one do with it, a vacant breath?
—We order potent spirits, with a nod
to Poe, his genius, drinking, raving death.

II
No music; cultured conversation in its hum
prevails. And no one's using a device,
manically thumbing, deaf and dumb,
confined in solipsistic paradise.

Outside, the wind is slipping over grass.
I feel its passing, dark—a raven's sign.
Enough; I shall not have a second glass.
The evening gathers all in its design,

as if—it's strange— the wing of poetry,
however grim the tale, or commonplace,
were beating at the portal. Words may be—
I pause—the medium of an eerie grace.

SONNET FOR PATRIC

The morning tennis ended after nine.
It's dry and warm, though not infernally.
No cold fronts, no AC—his taste, and mine,
from girlhood days. God's too—there's husbandry

in heaven. Pat prowls the cosmic library,
selecting titles, straightening a spine
— sufficient books for all eternity—
and, since it's not forbidden, drinking wine

of note, champagne, rosé, full-bodied red,
or Irish whisky. Later, music—song
(he knew 200), and his father's voice

joins in; Pat's own piano works. It's said
all tears are wiped away. He suffered long.
To each his own, in paradise. Rejoice.

Hit Man

The aging don of a Sicilian gang
is leaning on his squads, impatient youth
who send their threats on cell phones, like "Bang, bang"
for children playing with toy pistols. Truth

to tell, he doesn't want to lose control.
Those wise-guys clearly aren't what they should be!
Yet they would push him out, give him a roll
of bills, a tidy pad, and company

sometimes. Persuasion does no good, it seems.
With his credentials, what would one expect—
rough work, real murders, prison time, his dreams
fulfilled? He doesn't bother to reject

their arguments (untutored in debate).
So what are they to do? Abide until
he just drops out and joins the Syndicate
above? Or nudge him, with a codicil

of testimonies? But they lack the nerve
that he had when the stakes were high. A hit
man, then, professional, thereby to serve
their need at one remove, with benefit,

in fact, to him, unwilling sacrifice;
though surely never virtue's paragon,
he will atone a bit for family vice.—
Now, as for me, coeval to the don,

might fellow poets wish to bump me off,
some editor or upstart ready to assume
my place, for feeding at Euterpe's trough
too long, the classic figure in the room?

They'll have no cash to contract with a jobber;
they'll turn instead to green-eyed envy's fire,
death staged to seem the bungling of a robber.—
The bird of art will rise above my pyre.

Road Nostalgia

I'm suffering mightily for every mile
I will not drive again. Addicted, like
a smoker, gambler, drunk, I'll stop, though, while
I'm still ahead. Can we afford a spike

in tie-ups, crashes, loss of life and limb?
Do I want sirens, hot blue Cyclops lights,
crunched steel, flesh hanging from the bumper trim—
arrests, and someone reading me my rights?

It's true I won't miss freeway jams, delays,
construction zones, the fear I'll hydroplane
in downpours. No. But in my seeing days
I had hot love affairs with roads, two-lane

ideally, taking me through space and time
into myself. The desert! Ah, that drive
from Santa Fe—the upper Rio Grande, the climb
toward Taos, wrapped in sage, before the dive

down rapids, into sea-troughs, to salute
Arroyo Hondo, then regain lost height
at Questa! And that roller-coaster route
I took in Utah to Lake Powell! What might

the charioteers of old have thought (all men)?
One's so confined in circumstances. Give
to human freedom all its due: yet when
we view the scope of things, and how we live

so fugitively, shouldn't we devise
fresh ways of being? —Thanking God, I've quit
cold turkey, with my winnings. If I'm wise,
a different race will start. It's not yet "it."

KALE

What's this? New foodstuffs fans can rave about,
all green: chips, flatbread, pasta, rich with kale!
Perhaps old Popeye's spinach is worn out;
shiitake mushrooms, toney, are too pale

for folic acid; portobellos, tough
and brown, do not, I think, have chlorophyll.
And what of dandelions? Poor man's stuff,
suspect thereby, a garden weed, like dill.

And collard greens? A type of kale, in fact,
but southern, overcooked, with ham bone, salt—
ill-famed. Folk cooking's good, in the abstract;
but Dixie food partakes of Dixie's fault.

A salad made for the Thanksgiving feast
of cabbage, nuts, chopped kale, and who-knows-what
becomes the rage. The turkey, at the least,
deserves sincere appreciation—but

it looks and tastes as always. Novelty
and mania are key ingredients
in fashions; kimchi, fungi, bitter tea
can, oddly, turn into a preference.

A cheer for strange and rotten foods! Blue cheese
and tempeh, miso, sauerkraut—extremes
of tolerance, with tongue, radicchio; these,
with kale, prove sense cannot be what it seems.

EMBODIMENT

Philosophy's a useful enterprise
for mental workouts. It can soothe, console
(it's said) a downcast spirit, train the eyes
on the sublime, propose to make a whole

of fractured thoughts. What of the body, though—
that fellow-traveler with its own needs,
demanding, vulgar, ever quid pro quo,
companion without cease to thinking reeds?

We train *it,* too, of course, by exercise,
and groom it, like a cat. With lipstick, rouge,
good haircuts, stylish clothing, we disguise
most imperfections; every subterfuge

is fair. Just think: raw flesh, transformed, is served
at table; hands are seconded by forks
and knives, like ersatz body parts. Preserved
from wallowing, we sit up straight. Fat corks

are popped, enhancing meals (though may invite
wild interludes). We say "make love," to cover
what it really is, and hide the act at night,
pretending to the world no one's a lover.

Enough. All that's a clever *maquillage*
of earthiness and worse, the sticky real.
Philosophy sees through the camouflage.
We can't lie to ourselves, nor the ideal.

And this same body—only molecules—
contains a mind that then contains itself!
The back-and-forward never ends. We're fools
to think we can immobilize the elf

of logic and awareness. Being's the glue
within us. Try denying you're a lump
of clay—but where's pure thought, the pristine blue?
We must, as Montaigne said, sit on our rump.

"Turkey Vultures on a High-Rise Balcony." By Carol A. Miller.

Two Vultures

Perched on the broad railing of my balcony, they look huge!
I've never seen these creatures close at hand.
By highways, they are on the wing before the car arrives;
anyway, at the wheel, how could I stare? Still less
if they are circling. Yesterday, one came—a scout?—
flying up, or down, or landing by some chance (but what
can chance mean to a vulture?). Glimpsing it, surprised, I drew
away, observed discreetly, watched as it took cognizance

of its surroundings (but not of me), examining the balustrade,
a bench with pots, table, chairs, but fixing chiefly
on the sky, the street below, as if they could have altered.
Once or twice its hooked beak parted—
in a squawk? The bird seemed so uncertain of itself.
Might it be injured? But it flew off, well enough.
Today, it's brought its mate (Australian sense or reproductive,
I don't know). Side by side, now gazing downward,

now ahead, or toward each other, mirror images, they pass
the time. It's late November; surely they do not intend
to nest here! Again, I barely move, trying to remain unseen,
using angles, curtains. Now it's piano time,
though; what will they make of music? Slipping around
the long way to a corner, and turning on two lamps,
I seat myself. The vultures stay. It's Advent,
the first Sunday, opening the Christian year. Chords of grace

rise from my old hymnal: "Come, Thou Long Expected Jesus."
No reaction, none. I continue, inattentively,
far too distracted by the birds, whose heavy, feathered being
pulls at me. They seem very intimate, shoulders nearly
touching; they consult each other often, you
might say. Now and again they preen. The hymnal features
doves, of course, as Holy Spirit; Christ himself
refers to sparrows. But these black scavengers—what place

do they have in the divine Word? Yet they too must serve
in the ordained economy; all serve. Someone must clean up,
keep the road to Galilee fit for the Master.
The vultures perch for minutes more, paying no mind
to much except each other and the darkening clouds. Finally,
as I compose this, they are in the air, leaving, I trust,
no malediction, no ill omen, maybe even blessings—
strangely charged with testifying how God found creation good.

ALLY

It seemed I had no time when I was young
or barely felt it. It was just, alas,
a music worm, a melody unsung,
so faint I could not listen to it pass.

But, decades later, age seems on my side.
Time's spare now (little's left), but can be spared.
How hard and dense it was! First, student, bride,
apprentice teacher; long, professor, paired

with poet, plagued by deadlines, which distort
our senses. I would twist the hours, to wring
from them more potency and to assort
each effort to its end— that everything

be done, and nothing need survive on scraps
instead of close attention or embrace—
my family, students, writing, all, perhaps
at once. The film ran, as it were, in place.

I'm dancing with the years now, yours and mine,
my memories, my friends, the easy flow
of mornings, afternoons, and nights, a line
where sunlight dallies with the shade, a show

of purple in the sky, the buoyant sea,
which bears me, like Ulysses. What's ahead?
The rest, in its own time; for company,
two smiling angels and my cherished dead.

Three Arizona Poems

ARIZONA GRAPEFRUIT

In Ray and Sarah's Arizona patio, no limes will grow—
the elevation is five hundred feet too high;
but oranges, tangerines, and grapefruit flourish,
beautifully rounded (fruit, of course, but also trees).
The globes illuminate the dense green shade.
Every morning, Sarah steps outdoors to harvest grapefruit,
firm as softballs, halves them, gets out
her old-fashioned juicer, and *voilà*, the pale-yellow start

to breakfast. Doves nest thereabouts, inquiring "Who,
who?"; songbirds flit about, replying "We, we."
A fountain runs with music. Nearby
clumps of spiny, fibrous prickly pear and cholla. armed
with tiny, hairlike lasers, form fine *chevaux-de-frise*.
Admiring the grapefruilt once, a careless cousin
brushed an agave and found his wrist and arm attacked
by rapier tips *en garde*, which easily drew

blood; then, reeling, he fell sideways into prickly pear.
Tweezers were required, even the next day, for trousers
and the flesh itself. It's said a desert fruit tree
must be cleared around the lower trunk, its branches
trimmed, in order to discourage avian nesting
within range of snakes, which climb for eggs,
or raise themselves, as to a fakir. It's an old tale, the dyad
that engages beauty and the beast, not in competition

but allied, the better to deceive us, lure us, offering
jeweled pleasure-grottoes and lush gardens
where the rose in bloom seduces us, unfolding petals, red
on red, like lips, diffusing its enticing scent, thorns
at the ready; where blushing fruit, aglow
but, as we know, forbidden and thereby more beautiful,
awaits a candid hand. We're addicts of desire,
the wide world beckoning, its boundaries as if unreal.

"Saguaros." By Sarah Vesty.

Saguaros

Carnegiea gigantea is the name
(for Andrew C.). The species is unique.
As sentinels of Arizona's fame,
endowed with ruby fruit, a fine physique,

longevity, and patience, they gaze out
from shadowed eyes, where woodpecker and wren
have nested, on the desert seasons—drought,
monsoons in favored years. Their regimen:

luxurious sunshine, but economy
imposed for moisture, always. Eager cells
store quantities of water frugally
from snow and rain; the taproot draws on wells

and trickles. From their stance and steely spikes,
anthropomorphism leads me to conceive
an army on the hillside, halberds, pikes,
neat coats of mail, small weaponry. Naive.

Yet what can overcome the thought that man
and cactus may be kin? Form follows sense,
or offers it. Saguaros too began
from simple cells, evolved in time, ribbed, dense,

complex. I see them now, *en marche*, arms raised,
patrolling slopes and contravening trash—
defending nature for the world, amazed.
We'll join to curate beauty, with panache.

Canyon Loop Trail

—Catalina State Park

The Santa Catalina Mountains, to the east and south,
in early April still have streaks of snow.
Little green; if green comes, it will be a grace
of the monsoon in summer. This trail is lengthy,
rugged, steep, not fit for everyone. But at the outset
it's a gentle hike—more than a mile
of sandy surface, pocked in places, warty with rocks
elsewhere, crossed by tree roots, with inclines

and declines and a few stepping stones, and yet
within my range. A perfect morning! Sarah's
on a different trail with practiced mountaineers. So
off we go, Ray (giving up his workout)
and his two charges, lowland cousins, on the easier loop.
It's time to watch where I put down my feet;
but I must also study flora, take in the topography,
and admire the azure sky. Early signs of springtime

draw me—lupine and verbena. Saguaro, covering
a south-face hillside, won't show growth
until July, when the crowns will bloom. A little lizard
scampers through low brush, and birds are everywhere.
This is, as it were, a poem-trek, the rhythm
given bodily, the lines and diction shaped in dialogue
with desert spirits, which, passing by
as if appointed, I examine and interrogate. We cross

dry water courses, first a narrow gully, then a broad wash
redesigned by nature just last year, when rains
unseen for lifetimes overflowed the former banks,
enlarged the channel, and spread out still
farther, carrying and leaving rocks of many tons. Now,
we find smooth sand, and dry, essential thoughts,
almost mineral. Farther on, we pass
large swaths of blackened wood, where fire took

its pleasure lately; new forest, thicker, is in waiting.
How elemental all appears— nature
as the Greeks imagined it. The sky hits me, again,
with its blue hammer, and the sinuous sierra to our right,
cusps and saddles, flickers sunnily, a read-out
of my heart, its intermittences and its enduring
compass. How can we go further into the dark core
of this creation, its foundations, scope—no, into ourselves?

Affects

REGRET, I

A friend, coeval, asks what I regret
the most. Good land! Does he mean what I've *done*,
or, likely, have *omitted*? I can't let
myself inquire too long what laurels won,

what lost or scrapped. I surely was not kind
enough at times, a usual offence.
It's not true cruelty, but, rather, blind
misapprehension or indifference.

I know I've often wanted more than I
deserved, in patience, pardon. It's from greed,
a classic flaw; and others pay. And why?
They too are human, needy. But my need

came first. And what of opportunities
and gestures not acknowledged as one ought?
That chance to go to Spain one spring, those seas
unsailed, the handsome man. I could have bought

a little fishing ranch; it would have pleased
my father so. With exercise and rest,
would he have seen old age? I might have eased
my mother's widowhood. I failed the test

of true devotion more than once, it's clear.
What might have been I cannot bear to think;
the honored figures are no longer here.
It is too late, too late. My spirits sink,

then rise. Self-therapy? No, Christian sense;
experience, too. Shall I repeal the Fall?
I throw the dice again, for evidence.
Perhaps I'd do it over—most, or all.

REGRET, II

Memories sting, but, a seasoned masochist,
I cultivate them, stroke them as my progeny,
refine them, pouring on the acid of regret,
reliving what was lovely only to destroy
it by recalling what came after. I cannot

have hope; what's done is done; dead moments,
smiles, will not come back, nor I as what I was;
and so I flagellate myself to feel once more
the awful absence, parting, loss, the measure
of what might have been but can no longer be.

Regret, III

You should have come to join me right away,
while your desire was flying high,
at mast-top, and when I was smooth and navigable,
flowing toward you, into deeper waters
of full-bodied, even seas, lightly troughed

and crested, sunshine on point, subtle currents
and dark recesses below. And you must know it
now—practiced as you are, reflective,
self-possessed; and should have known it
then, proving my eyes, hearing my voice respond

uncommonly, then finding a small hand yielding
to yours, and two feet winging fast to follow
you. Who else would honor as I do all
you have been, the man, the mind entire, the books?—
The weather's changed. Goodbye, goodbye.

WRATH

Prefigured ominously by the gloom
that settles everywhere, a sullen face,
cold silence, seismic rumblings: with a boom,
his wrath erupts—by now, a commonplace—

and spews its lava. Reason has turned wild.
To shout, to shake in body, raise a hand,
take off a belt to terrify a child,
accuse absurdly, without cause, demand

responses to his charges is insane.
Is it cathartic? Does he get relief?
I barely breathe; my stomach and my brain
are cold. At best, the outburst will be brief;

but more may come. No beauty lies in ire,
no goodness. Truth, perhaps. So much the worse,
then, for it must be in our blood. A fire
of anger multiplies the human curse.

DREAD

That existential dread, poor Kierkegaard's foe:
we know it, even when we do not know
we know it. He acknowledged it; his life
was changed thereby. He sacrificed thus wife,
society, all peace of mind, the true,
according to the common human view,
the good, the beautiful. The fact of art
was but temptation, to be set apart;
morality, still incommensurate;
belief, impossible belief, his fate.
Thus nothing eased his stricken, angst-filled soul,
except renunciation of the whole,
with trembling of the body and the mind,
the fear of his damnation, and the bind
of self to *Deus absconditus*, God.
He could not live thus long, beneath the rod
of wrath against him and the mighty dread.
Did he rejoice to find that he was dead?

Joy

As waves, borne in by force and, pulsing, bear
their form until they break and foam on shore,
births, weddings, victories, an answered prayer
fulfill a vision that has come before.

Or else, a latent joy may wait in long
distress or ennui, its face concealed
as caution or vague hope. A scrap of song
may intimate the grace to be revealed

in time; or we just meet it at a turn
of heart or fortune, as the gods may choose—
a sudden sight, not happiness we earn.
Then, joy is ours to recognize, or lose.

Auld Acquaintance

For W. D. C.

So, my good friend broke his kneecap falling down
his steep back steps. That was last May. Now here I am, in late
September, in a grounded Air France plane in Paris,
waiting to take off, late, for Montreal, where we had planned
to meet; but, since he cannot come,
it's pointless now for me. The first surgery, he said, left him
in an awful dream of agony. The post-op period was lengthy,
painful, inconvenient—and ultimately, unproductive,

the patella, like a lazy clam, declining to close up.
Already he had cancelled flights to England and appearances
at a prestigious conference; and by July he knew
he couldn't take his long train journey to Virginia
and the Carolinas. What was to be done? Three re-assessments
(by new doctors); then a second surgery. He's out for weeks,
and Montreal was scratched, just like the others.—
So what am I about to do, flying there, without my friend,

whose company was the whole purpose of the visit—in the modes
of drinking, dining, seeing sights, and interpreting
for him? Why not change my travel dates, stay two more nights
in Paris, then fly directly home? Ah, here's the rub: as per
Air Canada, a change would mean a penalty, nearly
five grand, supposedly. Incredible. Protests were vain.
How well-timed, too: hah! I'm going where I do not want to go,
from an airport where controllers are on strike!—

true, an intermittent "stoppage"; worse thereby, however,
than if predictable. Yesterday flights were on hold, but then
resumed for certain routes and times, not all . . . not mine.
Without assurances, I sent an email to the Montreal hotel;
I'd not get there soon enough; I'd be a no-show. Yet
suddenly, today, Air Canada invites me to depart at once, despite
the strike! I gather wits and luggage, rush to find
a taxi, reach CDG.—What next? Air Canada has moved me

to Air France—a different hour, a different terminal! Somehow,
with my bad eyes, I make my way there, thrashing
through the dense and swirling crowds. In the plane, at last;
but at 2:00 controllers walk away again. Patience, patience . . .
Eventually, having made a point, they're back, and we fly
smoothly westward. But we're nearly three hours late,
and landing in Toronto! The new connecting flight to Montreal
has left long since. Yet, as per the ticket, I cannot stay here;

I must go on. Another change of terminal. Air Canada, again—
departing at 10:40. A twenty-four hour day. And no hotel;
what am I to do, sleep on a bench? Ah, Sylvia. Who is Sylvia?
My friend, to be commended. It's not too late in Texas,
and in Canada my phone will work! Quick, quick!
She bestirs herself, and just before I board she texts me:
I am booked now for two nights at the Airport Marriott.
It's an oasis! What a lovely bed! In the morning, coffee, roll;

more rest, then supper. No, I won't see anything of Montreal—
an airport apron doesn't count. I phone my hobbling friend
to let him know he's not forgotten. "How's your kneecap?"
"Better; this time it will heal, and therapy
is less like torture." Maybe he can go to Boston in November;
maybe I can visit him in Texas, stay at a nearby Hilton,
bemoan with him our lost adventure, while rejoicing
over *auld lang syne*. It's for themselves I cherish friends,

the cream and *la fine fleur* of many years. But also for myself,
for I am needy, too, as they must know. Have I thanked
them properly? I'll let them judge their sterling value
by the pains I take to see them, happy coin of love and loyalty:
in driving days, long trips through Texas, Colorado,
and New Mexico, even South Dakota; Greyhound busses, now,
or trains, or catching rides; planes to London, Paris, and New York;
oh, those hotels!—all to raise the cup of kindness, ever.

UNE JOIE UN PEU TRISTE

One is never so happy as in others.
—Joseph Conrad

Poe's "Nevermore," and Shelley's "sweetest songs"
for "saddest thought"—if trite and hyperbolic—
cannot be forgotten. Warm moments may turn inside-
out; wish-fulfillment fancies just collapse in ash. And yet . . .
and yet . . . We smile, we laugh, we look ahead,
imagine, dream; and we embrace, our arms encircling
one another and our future joys—children,
friendship, voyages, adventures—memories always

in mind. If cracks of bitterness appear on a smooth day,
or images, turned sour, change their meaning, look
for beauty. Here's another glorious sunset, golden rays
reflecting eastward onto cirrus layers, coloring
with today's affection what we envision for tomorrow.
Those clouds have kept their coral for long minutes!
The darkness at the edges is but *chiaroscuro.*
I turn to those I love, feeling a steady beat, sweet, sad joy.

ATTRACTION, I: A HAND ON MINE . . .

A hand on mine, an arm around my waist,
and, later, fingers riffling through my hair—
all welcome, or else terribly misplaced.
By chance, the two of us were, singly, there—

a crowded scene—but at the side, ideal
for making fast acquaintance. I'm reserved
by nature, cautious; but the man's appeal
had captured me. No doubt, I was unnerved,

and, loath to stay, still could not leave, in truth,
because he drew me back—a gesture, look.
Had I been magnetized somehow, for youth
to flow in me again? Or I mistook

myself, perhaps. Though Thanatos desires
us, greedy, Eros loves us well, and uses time
with skill to light astonishing new fires.
Deceit's impossible. Is love a crime?

ATTRACTION, II: WE'D MET THE DAY BEFORE . . .

We'd met the day before, for otherwise,
no story. Unaware, he was engrossed
in Etienne Gilson. "You get the prize,"
I thought, "for serious shipboard reading!" Most

one sees is common—cheap biography
or history, at best. A pint of stout
was still untouched. I stood there; would he see
or sense me? No; I had to draw him out,

return him to this world. I spoke. The smile
he gave me might have moved a stone; it moved
me, surely. Taking off his glasses, while
he stood and gestured toward the side, he proved

his pleasure: I sat down. The barman took
my order. "Cheers." We made a happy team—
for I disdain a man without a book,
and he got taste, consensus, and esteem.

IDYLLS IN THE MIND

They're cheaper, clearly, than a psychiatrist
or counselor of any kind, and much preferred, by me
at least, to suicide, and by my daughter,
Kate, her family, and friends, who care about me
and, I think, derive some pleasure from my letters,
parties, poems. For her, some future profit, too.
So to survive, I'll invent idyllic landscapes, skyscapes,
personages, bits of music, gentle action, smiles. Why not

begin tonight? I'll paint a Texas sunset, colored salmon,
mauve, and red, along a desert skyline
toward Twin Peaks and Paisano Pass. The work
is put away, the errands done, the heat dispersed. A breeze
has risen suddenly, My father's seated
on a bench, beside my mother, watching phoebes
arc their way toward darkness—though not yet. And I?
Anticipation. Peace settles on us, sociably,

with pleasing chuckles, observations, reminiscences,
emanations of refreshing thought. Much later,
company at evening on a Colorado balcony,
as broadening shadows climb the peak, the sky, ash blue,
the glorious cirrus. Different scenes: delights
with Houston friends, one afternoon, in their garden, palm
trees fanning us, the voice of time collected
in a tone that stirred the heart, aspiring. Elsewhere,

low, honeyed wall of stone around a plaza, holding sun,
providing its old wisdom. Another day, Kate and I
at a café terrace in New Orleans (if cafés are part
of idylls), happy, eating sliders, drinking wine.
Or lovers sailing on the ocean, spread before us,
bright pelt on a deep nothingness,
rippling its muscles, as we look out together,
mesmerized. Then an island rising; we step down

on sands of white, buy textiles in strong colors, bathe
in light that cleanses all. Here, take
my hand; lead me to a new *Arcadie*, where we belong.
Sweet music's playing, waiting for us, with a book,
a pen, these memories, and a drink called "Sunset,"
suiting those whose being, mellowed,
is attuned to one another's, magically, who love
with eyes and hand and tongue, ecstatic, yet serene.

ALIGNMENT

Think of wheels, even only two, on a bicycle,
or, for cars and trucks, your usual four,
six, and so on, up to twenty-two. Like us, a team.
Think of your spine, a serious matter, or an architect's
concerns, similarly crucial. All must be
coordinated—straight, or, for an ogee or rotunda,
beautifully curved, like arms. Too,
I have in mind, like Cassius, the weighty movements

in the skies, those heavenly alignments, mappable
motions of the spheres, reliable, until
a new star is created or old celestial fires
give out. My wheeling partner tells me we're "aligned."
What might he mean? Our birth dates
under the same zodiac sign, or a complementary
one? Fortunate conjunctions of key planets?
Likely, he pictures a more human scale,

the happy meeting of our tastes, our minds,
or the same faery dust that fell in the Bronze Age
on both our Irish bloodlines. Or he sees
that we are dancers in ordained arrangements,
circling, separating, meeting, never unaware,
never indifferent, no less together
when we align only by words across great distances,
our gravity holding one another well in place.

Abroad

LONDON . . . IF YOU CAN AFFORD IT

—September, 2021

Of course, the prices are quite high, despite
the drop in tourist trade. The pound outranks
the dollar. Still, at dusk I'll take a flight
there, get my yearly dose of pubs, the banks

of River Thames, the Tate, Museum Street,
Trafalgar Square. My flight's direct.
From Heathrow to hotel then, where I'll meet
a friend. It should be easy to connect.

Alas, I do not have a QR code
("What's that?") for vaxxing. Thus I cannot fly;
I'll stay and try tomorrow. This episode
may be an awful omen. Stuck, I sigh.

Next morning, hours and patience will be spent
in digital distress. But I depart,
at last. All London's lovely, as if meant
to compensate somehow and fill my heart:

green parks, fine churches, paintings, Shakespeare plays,
a gentle sense of time, the honored past.
We have survived the plague, in many ways,
and pleasures of this interlude will last,

the city scene, new friends, a four-course meal.—
It's time to leave. My vax card and the rest
are all in order, surely. Yet I feel
uncertain; something can go wrong ("the best-

laid plans . . .") Indeed, at Heathrow I must show
an eight-day Covid test. "But I'm exempted."
These papers, worthless? "Right; you cannot go
without it." Just remain? I might be tempted.

The cost of the hotel, museums, food
and drink is fair; I surely can afford
it. What's outrageous is the attitude,
the petty tyranny. I'm vexed, I'm bored,

delayed again, to get a nostril burn.
The plane for home has left; I'll spend a night
in Washington instead. Will I return
here, though? With joy; good Dr. Johnson's right.

At the Salisbury Pub

A party's going on, it seems. Often, perhaps, the Salisbury
is a party, drinkers filling rooms, spilling over
into St. Martin's Lane, flowing around Covent Garden,
stirring, pointillist. Pubs are usually masculine.
But this one is a *grande dame*, charming, well-preserved,
with ample life experience and an "interesting" past—
shadows, scars, a few notorious episodes. She still
looks good, her features opulent: fine carved mahogany,

glass, etched and polished, dark, massive bar, and nymphs
in bronze, of Art nouveau confection, holding lamps
designed as long-stemmed flowers. For notoriety,
old reminiscences of Oscar Wilde and homicides
remain, dim but persistent. No surprise;
the pub is more than centenarian, genuine Victoriana.
This evening there's no party, just the early crowd
straight from the office, young men, young women

greeting each other, kissing, pulling off jackets, pushing
tables together, ordering loudly at the bar.
So why am I here—foreigner, not employed at any office,
well past young? I'm not a stranger, though,
really, and though my "date," J.W., lives in Paris,
he likewise appreciates this town, where he has business.
We enjoy the place together, part of a yearly fix,
when we overdose on food, drink, art, and bookshops. Soon

he'll be back in France; another pal will come by train
from Sheffield. Who knows what beacons will light up
on our horizon? Is it too good, sybaritic? No;
it's grace—for me, for this old realm, a paragon
of civilized endeavor, under the sign of sacrifice
(think of Coventry, of streets here where V-2 rockets fell).
We drink up, head for an Italian restaurant,
hoping our friendly polities will flourish, love will last.

ALL SAINTS

A Gothic masterpiece—that's what I've heard—
a London gem, worth seeing. Off I go,
on foot, from Bloomsbury Street, quite undeterred
by unfamiliar districts. And I know

the way to Boots' at least: a chocolate bar,
a drink, a sandwich, to be saved. That done,
I head out, seeking shortcuts. Now, how far
is Margaret Street? The midday summer sun

is warm, the walkways crowded—jostling, dense
trajectories of boredom, need, desire.
At last, a signpost; now the route makes sense.
That slender cone must be the All Saints spire!

An entrance, narrow, hides in a façade
of claret hue. The handle turns; I find
a courtyard, gables, arches, vaguely odd.
It's *1850s* Gothic!— well designed,

a High Victorian phenomenon.
All's polychrome: bright egg-yolk yellow tile,
red brick, black bands, a modern paragon
of money married to medieval style.

Inside, it's geometrically ornate,
to praise the God of order, who made man
and beauty. Wood, gilt, paintings celebrate
His grace. I spot the Pious Pelican.

I have my lunch outside, along a wall
of flowers, near a little palm tree. Birds,
Christ's darlings, flit about. The ancient Fall
is far away, redeemed, like flesh, by words

and suffering, which, somehow, must prevail,
though immaterially, conjoined with bone,
blood, water, as the living Holy Grail.
I turn to leave, and brush the cornerstone.

BELFAST

—September 2022

Free busses furnished by the locals take us from the dock,
the top deck giving ample views. Clear skies today;
the rain that fell for hours in the Republic does not bother us
up here, We are deposited near the town centre,
our eyes directed to the City Hall, magnificent. And here's
a Hop-On bus—a one-pound fare, a friendly driver
who insists he's not a tour guide but has been one,
and who knows his city. First, the Belfast Lough, the harbour,

quays, light industry; then off to the "districts" and their gory
history, from the great division of the island
in the twenties—such a long, unhappy, seething co-existence—
to the thirty years of "Troubles" and a city split in two. Oh,
the pity of it all! The Hop-on bus turns west,
along Falls Road and endless "Peace Walls," at the interface
of urban warfare, once. Imagine: boundaries uncertain;
soldiers under oath, with fire power; clandestine forces,

even more determined, made of fierce men and boys,
with bombs (often blown up with them); bullets flying wildly
across streets, as in Beirut, Berlin; deaths provoked
by emblems, colors, speech; and babes in arms, young widows
nursing vengeance maybe, vowing to remember all
and risk it all again. These memorial signs are hortatory
too: the wounds are deep, the new skin fragile. Don't they invite
new outbreaks, those clenched fists and phrases of rebellion,

against those, anywhere, who may prefer a proven order
to long anarchy, the Terror, the Commune? This protest line's
the longest in the world. When, by other roads, we're driven
toward the east, I barely can admire the architecture—new
buildings, jewels of the past: Queen's University
(Victorian) and other styles with royal names. Subdued,
I must breathe deeply of what passes now for peace, and marvel
at the City Hall again, a masterpiece in marble, crystal,

and dark wood (good public toilets too). At a pub, we chat
with the lovely Irish waitress, of porcelain complexion. Time
to go back to the pier, the ship. On board, I choose
a better shirt for dinner, get a place then at the bar.
The telly's showing women's rugby. Suddenly, a voice,
most solemn, interrupts the play: the Queen has died. Long live
these Isles, their suffering soul. "My dear mama, my dear
papa," says King Charles. Might blood, sense, Christ prevail?

In the Twelfth Arrondissement

—Paris

I
It's nearly new to me, this awkward wedge,
the largest segment of the spiral shell
defining Paris. At the eastern edge
lie Saint-Mandé, Vincennes. A sentinel—

a monumental column—marks northwest,
where the Bastille gave up a few insane,
unruly prisoners, a palimpsest
in bodies, stone. Perfumes of time remain,

despite the modern opera house, immense.
A station's near. Three tourists with their maps,
their fanny-packs, pass by; the crowds are dense.
For some, though, this is home. —Look! Those, perhaps,

are Sunday mariners, who've moored their boat
among the vessels of the "Arsenal," a port,
which we admire along the quais, afloat
in sun. —Now, toward the islands! which assort

their harmonies of architecture, tree,
and bridges to our taste. Tonight we'll dine
in brick arcades, a nineteenth-century
construction for a busy railway line,

repurposed as a promenade, all green
on top; beneath, shops, studios, a café,
and *L'Arrosoir*. What elegant cuisine!
We'll not forget the "Twelfth" and its bouquet.

II
Yes, Paris is all light, in autumn sun;
its monuments are radiant. What's done
is done. But can we recognize our bond
with history—ourselves—yet go beyond

it, both in honor, due, and due regret?
Consider just two centuries, the net
of revolutions: after the Bastille,
the guillotine and the Hôtel de Ville,

where Robespierre was seized in '94;
rebellions and repressions, fire and gore,
two monarchies, two empires, war, Commune,
starvation, anarchy. And still the tune

may echo: formal minuets for flute,
"La Marseillaise."—Fear power; tame, dilute,
confine it. Others' eyes are watching. Love
these fine arcades, the verdant path above.

A Gallery

WOMAN WITH MOP AND BUCKET

She's smocked in blue, like peasants by Millet
at work, a crook or pail in hand, or bent,
perhaps, for sewing, nursing, sheaving hay,
their faces worn by pity and consent.

The airport crowds have atomized by now;
the loos are nearly empty. There, alone,
she traces arcs, a model showing how
it's done—left, right, ahead—as if to hone

her gestures as a dance routine. She sings,
a thread that rises, falls, and floats.
The words are muffled. Might her voice give wings
to home thoughts, in its melancholy notes?

I speak to her in English; no reply,
no recognition. I use Spanish then;
she's pensive, unaware. So should I try
my Creole French?   But no; to speak again

would seem interrogation. Does she see
me, even, leaning as she swirls her mop?
She is the body of the melody,
its mute existence when the song must stop.

FULL MOON PARTY

A "souvenir" from several years ago.
Pat's still alive; we've started on a cruise.
A Full Moon Party is announced—a show
of sorts—on deck fourteen. That is good news,

for he's a fan. At night, a mirror in hand,
he rises to observe her, high above
him, at an angle. What can make him stand
for minutes thus, pyjama-clad, in love

with that bright orb, so mythic, so admired?
—He's Celtic, not adverse to lunacy.
So we'll attend the party, though quite tired,
expecting whimsy, song, and poetry.

The lunar centerpiece will be here soon,
we hope. The orchestra, the staff, the host
await the lamp that seems so opportune
for sailing. "Bon voyage!," a champagne toast.

Few travelers gather, though; will scanty crowds
suffice to honor her at this late hour?
The cosmic timer ticks. And will the clouds
cooperate? We've had an evening shower.

Oh, think of Turner's Milbank scene!—the play
of light on ripples, trees, a single spire
above the city line, and the array
of boats and sails, beneath the moon on fire.

"Artemis may be rising!" someone's cried.
A sense of glow develops—in my mind?
She's shadowy still, as if she wished to hide.
But what's that yellow there—a lemon rind?

If so, she should emerge now, swell, explode
as orange, then gold, then silver-white, to climb
and ride in majesty her cosmic road.
But all is black. The moon can take its time,

but Pat and I cannot; the supple cord,
once long, is running out. The party's quite
a flop. An evening's loss—we can't afford
it! So adieu, coy goddess, and goodnight.

Photograph by Dorothea Lange. Taken in the Texas Panhandle.

DUST BOWL

Alone, a woman stands in black and white
surveying a discolored sky above
and nothing on the earth around her, save
a windmill, with its blades congealed on film,

vain, futile. Pride has not deserted her,
her stance proclaims; but she has nothing else—
no hope, and no defiance possible.
Despair inhabits her; a hand may start

to sketch a gesture, loosely, but it falls
in uselessness. Her eyes, whatever hue
in fact, are dark; her face is drained of all
futurity, as arid as the soil.

To act is meaningless; the land resists
whatever project that she might conceive.
Her husband, children—absent from the scene
of tragedy. She bears it all, arms crossed.

STILL LIFE

Tomorrow friends will gather here, at five
or so. A simple *vin d'honneur*, a way
to celebrate the fact that we're alive.
I ironed a yellow tablecloth today,

and bought, to fit a Steuben bowl, fresh fruit,
as centerpiece; I'll add a cutting board,
a knife, a spread of cheeses that will suit
most tastes. The eyes will linger—the reward

for knowing Chardin's canvasses, the shine
of goblet, pearly onion, and a half-
peeled lemon, lustrous grape, or clementine,
the drape of linen napkin, a carafe.

Raw nature and our needs propose a start;
we go beyond, to work, by providence,
a transformation of the world in art,
reflecting back fresh beauty, altered sense.

LEFT BANK BOHEMIAN

Long, stringy hair (combed when? when washed?), dyed black
(blond roots still show); drab skirt; brown Birkenstocks—
a charming sight. She's modern—won't look back
to former usages, professions, clocks.

But she's creative, doubtless, loves all art,
devours "ideas," has sketches, plans, a draft.
To live by reason would betray her heart.
She doesn't know that *art* begins by *craft*.

She strolls along Boul' Mich', sits in cafés,
meets strangers, and collects a vital store
of passions, feelings, lust, and daring ways
to shock—transgressively, self-metaphor.

True difference may elude us in its guise
of fad. In any case, Apollinaire,
Fauves, Cubists, and Surrealists took the prize
a hundred years ago for novel fare.

She says all chains, all limits should be burst.
A boundary's the enemy, to her.
Yet untamed impulses become dispersed.
Think how a piston needs a cylinder.

I could not do without her, though—the yang
of energy that complements my yin,
Apollo's needed opposite, the Bang
of Dionysus and his drunken kin.

I'm drawn, despite myself, to pallor, kohl,
the unconventional, the rebel kind.
A Left Bank dynamo, a seething soul
may prove the matrix of a classic mind.

Rain

—New Orleans

How strange when moments come around again.
Perhaps it's *déjà vu, déjà vécu*, just slightly off. Am I
fatigued? Or, rather, circumstances turn,
and an experience is renewed but in a different key.
Trying to dry off, I'm seated in a restaurant, "Poseidon,"
at the bar, mirrored. Through the rows
of bottles, I see outward, since, behind me likewise,
all is glass. Rain is streaming down, and around us

night wraps, thickly, yet sensations rush in thicker yet—
wet sounds (tires smacking in the puddles, a muted horn)
and sights (low beams swimming on St. Charles Avenue
or turning in for take-out; bicycle lamps,
just points of light; streetcars all aglow, their windows
steamed, blurred images from the hotels and bars
across the way). On foot, a cluster of determined
tourists wearing plastic hats and raincoats push ahead,

some brandishing umbrellas, weaponizing them
against the slanting downpour. An ill-clad old fellow
has one, too, found maybe in a gutter, askew
and with bent ribs. Oh, it's Paris for me,
in a darkened mode, again. I remember dripping walks
along the quais beside the *bouquinistes'* and up
the Boulevard St.-Michel —black umbrellas thrust
aloft, as in canvases by Gustave Caillebotte;

leaves, discolored, slippery underfoot; and how wind
tossed and scattered scraps of paper, damp, broken wings,
dropped or blown from rubbish bins—bills, drafts
of poems maybe, letters, swirling round—
their messages in someone's head or heart, or lost
entirely, their appeals for aid, their desperate cries
of homesickness or love washed out, dead echoes, now
reanimated, painted in my mind forever.

AT THE BAR IN THE ENSEMBLE LOUNGE

It's open to both sides. No mirror, unlike
Manet's "Folies Bergère," but muted glow.
One stool is free, the evening's lucky strike.
Or is it? She inquires. "Yes." And so

they're thrown together, in a melody
for two, of talk, desire. He's muscled, trim,
smooth-faced, intelligent—and handsome; she
is lithe and lissome, in his words. The dim

illumination helps her. Each has wit
to offer, with a manner that bespeaks
wide reading and good judgment. Thus they fit
each other's taste, it seems. But in her cheeks

great age has chiseled hollows; lines traverse
her forehead. Soon enough she must reveal
an awkward fact. She sees it could be worse;
he finds time's writing adds to her appeal.

ISLANDS RISING

We've slept so well we're just now out of bed.
I draw the curtain back to greet the day,
and look straight out, then skyward, then ahead,
and there three islands rise, not far away,

the forms emerging, shaking off the night,
round hips and shoulders, hollowed dark in green,
and breasts, erectile, aureoled in light.
This port call, now, unsettles me; the scene

of sun on water, the volcanic cones
in outline pull me strangely, as obverse
to memory. The desert!—blanched-out stones
and sand, arroyos, mesas that disperse

to the horizon, scree of lava piled
around us. Those three hills that Georgia saw,
then painted, near Alcade, treeless, wild,
irreal somehow, symmetrical, but raw—

they're here, transfigured as a darker dream.
And what are we? I want to understand
how bodies fit their other selves, the stream,
the sweep of emptiness that proves the land.

Eleven Poems on Cocktails

OLD FASHIONEDS

Aunt Flora learned to drink them rather late,
but not *too* late. They carried her away
delightfully. She would not hesitate
to have a second, even third. She'd say,

"Don't spare the bourbon; extra sugar, please."
Her agèd muscles tightened, and her wit,
concise and pointed, flourished with fresh ease.
"A second cherry also." In a bit,

she'd start a joke, the shaggy-doggie type,
enchanting us, although we knew it well
already. Just her smile and gestures—hype
not needed—made it new and fit to tell

again. She nearly danced, her little feet
alive with pleasure, every charming pound
(not quite one hundred) lively, in a neat
circumference. She'd sip her drink around

the bar, eat (sparingly), then work the room.
Where were her melancholy then, her years
in bed, the somber winter, Celtic gloom?
Old miseries had melted in the cheers

of friendship and high spirits. Thank the Lord
for whiskey if it filled that ruined lung
with oxygen, expanding the accord
of breath and heart that almost made her young.

THE *BOULEVARDIER*

—2022

A Baton Rouge acquaintance sighs: "Back when . . ."
He means the lockdown, isolation, rage,
strange habits, forcibly, strict regimen.
Confined, he and his wife turned up a page

or two in some bar manual from France,
with recipes and variants to last
for weeks. Each day, they took a chance
on novelty—a relic from the past

or just a fad. Why not a *boulevardier*?—
exotic, from a different country, style
of dress, age, politics—a distant day.
Three liquors furnished flavors to beguile

the time. And no need for sobriety;
with everything shut tight, where would they drive?
No boulevard to stroll; no play to see.
Rejoicing simply that they were alive,

they filled their glasses with the liquid stuff
of pleasure and *détente* for evening hours
together; tasty dinners then, enough
to feed them and defy the reigning powers.

Nostalgia for such dreadful times is odd,
but good; it proves a gentle victory.
They thank each other warmly and thank God,
who kept them in high spirits, company.

LEMON-DROP MARTINIS

—For C. A. M.

A neighbor, Carol, has invited me
for drinks. Her charming daughter Lynn is there,
from Costa Rica, where she surfs. The sea
has left its azure in her eyes; her hair

reflects the light. She knows the recipe
for lemon-drop martinis, drinks with flair—
the curling lemon peel, its pungency,
Cointreau, sweet syrup, vodka—debonaire.

The shaker's cold already. She adds ice
and turns it gently with a chemist's skills,
then strains and pours the mix (she is precise

with liquids) into frosted glasses. Chills
of pleasure follow— for the eye, the tongue.
We're surfing in sensation, sunny, young!

Sazeracs

My foreign visitor wanted us to walk from Baronne Street,
through the lobby of the Roosevelt Hotel. A whole
block long, it's elegant: fine chandeliers, historic tiles,
plush seats, and sparkling Christmas decorations
then. He barely looked. For what he wanted was to meet
the manager to say that he, my visitor, had stayed there once
some forty years before. To whom the honor
went was clear enough. We saw the famous Blue Room

and stepped into the bar, where, despite the price,
he ordered sazeracs, not remembering them, but realizing
they were the barroom's eponym and they were famous,
created in New Orleans—he'd brag on them at home.
The angostura bitters hit him He scowled, made
a wry face, but pretended to be charmed. *He* paid, of course—
it was his caprice. We dined that evening at Café Degas,
my treat. No sazerac. He asked for Wachau Valley

wine. The owner's from Lausanne. At least she knew
the Austrian name, but had none. French, then. As a starter,
he chose *assiette de charcuterie*. Quite a display, enough
for three. Then *vichyssoise*. More wine. The next evening,
he was on his own. He'd manage; his hotel
was on St. Charles near others, bars, and restaurants.
I gave suggestions. What did I learn later? He'd walked
into the Pontchartrain and crashed a private party! No shame

either; he emphasized how he had drunk and eaten liberally.
That's not all. The following day we queued up to take
a river boat downstream an hour, then back. He was impatient
in the line, tried to jump it, and took great offense
when he was told to wait. He yelled an epithet no one should use.
Scarlet with embarrassment, I apologized for him. On the boat,
more boorishness. But at the bar, I spoke up first
and ordered sazeracs, "with extra bitters for my foreign friend."

POÈME-COCKTAIL

My little bar is nearly bare; there's just
pink grapefruit juice and wine. Not much,
if others were to come. They won't, I trust.
I'll use imagination, with a touch

of lunacy. The ice goes first—a few
half-moons; then juice (at least an ounce or so),
then wine. This French *fond de bouteille* will do—
still good, a fresh and lively white Bordeaux.

I do not stir the mix, but gently swirl
the glass to give momentum to the ice.
It works: the strata last, while droplets pearl.
To live, to drink, to write: a cast of dice.

I add an image and two lines of verse
to give the contents soul. One could do worse.

DRY MARTINIS

—In memory of J. P. H.

We're out in Taos, my cousin John and I, to join
his sister Edith and her husband for three days
before we leave to camp in Arizona. We can't stay
with them; they have an A-frame house,
one room at the top; below, a tiny kitchen and the office,
where he runs his on-site business. So,
we'll bed down tonight at the old Sagebrush Inn, south
of town, authentic. Outside, weathered adobe walls,

not concrete painted over; venerable cactuses
and shrubs; and towering cottonwoods. Inside,
huge ponderosa *vigas* at the ceiling, lots
of space, all well designed, with pueblo rugs, dark wood,
and souvenirs— of artists, R. C. Gorman,
Ansel Adams, Georgia O'Keefe; of boys and teachers
from Los Alamos, refugees in '44; a U.S. president;
and sundry actors. There's an ample bar,

as you'd expect. Here we are, then, having driven
northward from El Paso, through Moriarty
and Las Vegas, at the speed of western winds. Time
for a drink, before we meet the others. "Dry martinis,"
orders John. Now, he's a sturdy man, robust;
his embonpoint is clearly visible. He
can take his cocktails, easily. I'm not built that way.
Still, I yield. Oh, my! This bartender knows his trade,

and, since no one else is here, he does not hurry.
What a classy drink, to match the art!
Dear John's a family doctor, father of six children, too;
he deals in realities. He announces, "A martini's
like a woman's breasts. One's two few, three too many."
Right away Picasso comes to mind, his *demoiselles*,
their misshaped attributes in frontal view
and profile, multiplied. John has a second drink,

but I decline. We leave for dinner (blue corn enchiladas,
salsa verde). Camping will be perfect,
with smooth sand underfoot, guardian trees, no rain. —
At home this evening, by myself, I'll make dry martinis—
two—and think of how so many years ago
John, driving home from Taos, died alone of septicemia
in a run-down roadside motel in East St. Louis, Illinois—
no jokes, no alcohol, no purchase left on life at all.

PROSECCOS

—*For T.*

"I'll have what she is having." That's his style.
"Prosecco," says the barman; "you can't miss."
I turn; we greet each other with a smile,
a gesture of delight, a telling kiss.

A diamond day. The sun's descending fast,
though, now—dark, crimson fruit that earth devours.
A toast to us. Let's make the evening last,
imprint it with a language that is ours

alone. The bubbles tickle down my throat.
Another glass, then dinner. We agree:
proseccos, laughter, kisses all promote
the sureness of our new-found company.

SUNSETS

How could I not include this drink,
since sunsets (visible or virtual) end everything
on every day, over and over? As with the real event,
a sunset in a glass has variations,
geographic (the generic tropical, the Malibu,
and the Italian, with amaretto), liquors (vodka, rum,
tequila, the aforesaid amaretto), garnishes
(nearly any fruity bit that fits the rim), but always

the crucial grenadine. To stir or not to stir?
The heavy grenadine may be mixed in,
or, better, left to fall through thinner liquid
and the ice, to settle in a layer of flaming scarlet,
as at the horizon. "Sunrise" drinks,
a counterpart, are much the same, but are, ideally,
stained with grape juice or dark cherry, rivaling
the russet mantle of the dawn, or crushed strawberry

for palest pink. They're good for hangovers, it's said—
starting afresh. Some have yoghurt, even. Ah,
the syrup of pomegranate seeds, belovèd
of the desert tribes—the fruit of Demeter, Proserpine!
It goes beyond its rough exterior; those red grains
explode in pleasure in the mouth. At sundown
once, a special being ordered for me that concoction,
fitting to the scene, which I sipped sparingly,

prolonging color and sensation, preserving moments
in that glass of wizardry for sweet enjoyment, *lento*
and *cantabile*. I picture it not as an end
but a beginning, as an hourglass turning over, filling
more than once with visions. What
an expanse within the human heart! Tell me again
how we can stroll together there,
at ease, embracing all we've known, and the yet-to-be.

Manhattans

—For T. M. B.

His eyesight's bad, his hearing, too; his knees
cannot be trusted, whence a wheeled device
to lean on; and a puzzling nerve disease
leaves fluid to be drained. Not very nice.

Tonight, we'll disregard how he has changed,
as we raise toasts to this old friend of mine
—his natal day. His wife's got all arranged.
No gifts, she said; but I've brought rosé wine,

and he will make Manhattans. Gone is youth;
to measure well is hard, but he can feel
the weight— delighting as the sweet vermouth
meets whiskey, bitters, strips of lemon peel.

A younger doctor, seeing him, might think
it is too much; he'll hasten death thereby.
So much the better, maybe; have a drink,
another, laughing, happily; then die.

I'd not refuse to write my final act
that way. By chance, I turn, among the crowd,
to face a mirror, and glimpse an artefact
so striking that I nearly cry aloud,

but stop—that agèd personage is I,
coeval with my friend. Who else is here?
A generation hanging on. But why
hang back? Life's precious. Spend it well, and cheer.

KILLER MARTINIS

I'm in a patio with my agèd friend
and Lina, his amanuensis. Yew,
espaliered, covers walls; great oaks extend
their limbs, like Hindu dancers, toward the blue

of springtime. Lina brings a healthy tray
of veggies, with blue cheese, and takes requests
for drinks. "Oh, just a spritzer, please, today."
My host has other notions; he suggests

I try a new *apéritif.* "You must!"
"I must?" I'm mulish; why should I agree?
But we are longtime friends; I trust
and want to humor him. He adds, "You'll see."

He likes a little glass, his cocktail neat.
I choose dilution, so I ask for ice.
"What's this—the flavoring? It's slightly sweet."
"Oh, wine." I sip again. It's rather nice,

but I'm unsure. "A Riesling, pinot gris,
shiraz?" "It's killer wine, a toxic yeast
that can resist infection easily
and prospers, multiplying. Once released,

it may kill off the better strains of stuff
or fight disease instead." "For goodness' sake,
let's change the subject."—I have had enough!
For me, the viscera are hard to take,

and I don't want strange medicine with food,
nor classes on bacteria. In truth,
this "killer" drink just doesn't fit my mood.
The classic next time—gin and dry vermouth.

Mimosas

—*New Orleans*
—*For K. E. D. and C. C. D.*

The three of us have met for Carnival.
Kate, born here, needs to get her native fix.
I often come, my home a corpuscle
of real estate. Add Clara. Happy mix,

with lovely weather and the easy reign
of fools. At lunch, mimosas are the choice—
the orange juice freshly squeezed, enough champagne
to foam, the frothy "Pfft," the very voice

and taste of sunshine—plus a local treat
(authentic accent, courtesy, and wit
itself) when suave René comes by to greet
us in his rounds. A charmer. He can fit

his words to anyone. "What have we here?
Fine ladies! Welcome! Oh, what family style!
Mimosas!" Quick: he takes my hand—no fear
of outraged feminism—with a smile.

We sip our drinks and chat throughout the meal
(shrimp Louie and fried oysters, dirty rice)—
we three, the city in a commonweal,
mimosas as our memory's device.

ENDNOTES

"Scythe." The critic and journalist is Danny Heitman, editor of *Phi Kappa Phi Forum*, a columnist for the Baton Rouge *Advocate*, and a contributor to the *Wall Street Journal*.

"Swan Boats." This poem echoes loosely certain elements of Tchaikovsky's *Swan Lake*. Readers may think also of Wagner's *Lohengrin*. The dedicatee is John William Corrington, the fine poet and fiction writer from North Louisiana.

"Dinner at Gautreau's." The poet Jules Supervielle (1884-1970), on whom "Laine" wrote her dissertation, was born in Montevideo of a French banking family. As an infant, he was taken by his parents to France, where both died that same year. Reared by an uncle and aunt in Montevideo and believing himself to be one of their children, he discovered belatedly that his real parents were dead. He was haunted throughout the rest of his life by a sense of loss. Each of his sailings across the Atlantic (more than a score) was for him a re-enactment of the primordial arrival, then deprivation. See likewise my poem "Carolina," based on a true story from South Carolina, in *The Muscled Truce*.

"Napoleon House." The story of Girod's planned expedition to rescue the captive emperor seems to be unsubstantiated; but it persists, and no evidence against it has appeared.

"Among the Muses." In New Orleans, the final *e* of *Calliope, Euterpe, Melpomene*, and *Terpsichore* is silent (as in French), thus reducing the syllable count from that usually heard in America. In this poem, the standard *e* sound is restored for the beat.

"Anthony and Cleopatra." The sonnet is dated 1884. Born in Cuba of a Spanish father and a French mother, Heredia was educated partly in Paris and lived there as an adult.

"The Conquistadors." From *Sonnets et eaux-fortes*, 1869. This translation follows the rhyme scheme exactly and uses many of the lexical elements found in the original. Heredia translated the preface to *Historia verdadera de la conquista de la Nueva España*, 1630, by Bernal Díaz del Castillo. This poem refers loosely to that text. The stars would not, literally, rise in the west. The poet simply alludes, presumably, to constellations, such as the Southern Cross, visible as the ship navigates in a southwesterly direction. Given the date of the poem, the use of *montage* is anachronistic, if its first appearance was early in the twentieth century, as sources say. Heredia's own liberties in writing of stars make this poetic license minor.

"The Sound of the Horn." This sonnet, published in 1881, has obvious echoes of Alfred de Vigny's poem "Le Cor" (1826), the last line of which is "Dieu! que le son du cor est triste au fond des bois!" That poem refers back to the famous episode of the horn in *La Chanson de Roland*. Verlaine's sonnet is reminiscent also of Vigny's "La Mort du loup" (1843). Throughout, insofar as possible, this translation uses Verlaine's lexicon, in which some choices may appear surprising, e.g. "barking," "drowsy," "lint," "mildness." The rhyme scheme is his.

"Hunting Horns." Published first in *Les Soirées de Paris*, 1912, then in *Alcools* (1913). The rhyme scheme is Apollinaire's, as is the use of short lines and the absence of punctuation, which he deleted on the proofs of *Alcools*.

"Poems in the Manner of Yüan Hung-tao." Yüan Hung-tao (1568-1610) was a major poet of the Ming dynasty. See Jonathan Chaves, ed. and trans., *Pilgrim of the Clouds: Poems and Essays from Ming China* (New York/Tokyo: Weatherhill, 1978).

"Moon Tracks." The footnote, while in the style of genuine footnotes in Professor Chaves's volume (see above), is facetious—a sort of poet's joke—but, of course, not in mockery of him.

"Things I've Seen at Carnival." "Cherry-pickers"—electric company repair and tree-trimming trucks—go along parade routes in advance of the high floats to make sure that no limb from the historic oaks on St. Charles Avenue has fallen or leaned enough to create a danger.

"Hit Man." Information on the central figure comes from an article on organized crime in New York, in the *Wall Street Journal*, 5 October 2021, 10. "'They certainly don't kill people like they used to,' said a former FBI agent."

"Embodiment." This poem holds echoes, obviously, of Montaigne (*Essais*, Book III, 13), Pascal's *Pensées* (the thinking reed), and Sartre (the viscous in *L'Etre et le néant* and *La Nausée*). The use of the term *the blue* (*l'azur*) to indicate the ideal was illustrated particularly by the poet Stéphane Mallarmé.

"Saguaros." The species is the only one in its genus. Standing saguaros are protected by law. Fallen saguaros are not, but perhaps they should be, since fallen and decaying specimens contribute to other organic life. The blossom is the state flower of Arizona. Saguaros grow only in the Sonoran Desert: in Mexico, southern Arizona, and a part of California. Yet their familiar silhouette often serves as an emblem of the Southwest in general.

"Canyon Loop Trail." Such abundant rains had last fallen in the 1880s.

"Auld Acquaintance." The airport codes mentioned are Dallas-Fort Worth and Charles de Gaulle.

"*Une Joie un peu triste.*" The poem title and the epigraph, both originally in French ("*On n'est jamais si heureux que dans les autres*"), come from Conrad's letters of 20 August 1919 and December 1920 to André Gide, *Correspondance*, ed. Pierre Masson and Jean-Pierre Wittman, *BAAG*, no. 213-14 (Spring 2022), 68, 77.

"A Hand on Mine." In addition to following generally the *carpe diem* poetic trope of the Renaissance, this poem echoes, loosely,"*To His Coy Mistress,*" by Andrew Marvell.

"London . . . If You Can Afford It." The allusion is to Samuel Johnson's pronouncement that "a man who is tired of London is tired of life."

"All Saints." The name *All Saints*, when used with *church*, *priory*, etc., seems to be spelled today without the apostrophe. Boots, Ltd., is the dominant drugstore presence in UK.

"Belfast." Although suggesting the general situation in Belfast as it is today, this poem cannot take into account the friction and practical difficulties produced by the Brexit vote and subsequent negotiations over borders and tariffs among the United Kingdom, the Republic of Ireland, and the European Union.

"In the Twelfth *Arrondissement.*" The islands are *l'Ile de la Cité* and *l'Ile Saint-Louis* in the Seine. This poem supposes a rough dialectical sense of history, but not that of Hegel or Marx. The railway station mentioned is the *Gare de Lyon*. It is not connected to the old viaduct formerly carrying the elevated railway (Paris-Bastille -Vincennes). The viaduct, saved from demolition by neighborhood supporters and the City of Paris, was repurposed to create the *Viaduc des Arts* (opened 1989). The project, undertaken by the Socialist government (1981–95) of François Mitterrand, was among his eight grand projects; one other, the Ministry of

Finances, is likewise in the Twelfth. The use of the former arches to create spaces for artists and artisans is a reminder of the historical prominence of craftsmen in the district; they were, traditionally, independent-minded. The *Coulée verte*, the promenade built on top of the arcades, which farther east descends to ground level, was finished by 1993.

"Left Bank Bohemian." Though a contemporary figure, with her Birkenstocks and "theory," this Bohemian, like others today, brings to mind those of the nineteenth century as depicted in prose, famously, by Henry Murger in *La Vie de bohème* and *Scènes de la bohème* (1849, 1851) and by Henri Daumier and others graphically.

"A Hand on Mine . . ." The phrase *great age* is borrowed from a repeated line in *Chronique* (1959) by the French poet St-John Perse (Alexis Leger).

"Islands Rising." The painting in question is Georgia O'Keeffe's *New Mexican Landscape, 1930.* The adjective *irreal*, while absent from standard dictionaries, has, along with the noun irrealism, varied uses now among philosophers and aestheticians.

"Old Fashioneds." Readers of *Arm in Arm* (2022) will recall the sonnet *"Heart,"* tracing briefly my aunt Flora's illness. See also "Aunt Flora Through My Retroscope," *Phi Kappa Phi Forum*, Fall 2021, 18-20.

"The *Boulevardier.*" The word has only three syllables in French. Initially, it referred to a man-about-town or *bon vivant*, especially an *habitué* of the cafés and restaurants along the post-Haussmann boulevards of late nineteenth-century and early twentieth-century Paris. The drink seems to have been concocted in the 1920s.

"*Poème-cocktail.*" This sonnet alludes obliquely to Stéphane Mallarmé's *Jamais un coup de dés n'abolira le hasard* and Guillaume Apollinaire's form called *poème-conversation.*

"Dry Martinis." In 1944, the Manhattan Project took over entirely the site of the Los Alamos School for Boys. The U.S. president was Theodore Roosevelt. The cousin mentioned is John Paul Hill (1927-1992).

"Sunsets." The Old Testament contains numerous allusions to pomegranates, in the Song of Solomon and elsewhere. The use here of "explode" echoes the military meaning of *grenade.* There is likewise an echo of the free-verse poem "*Ronde de la grenade,*" by André Gide, which became part of *Les Nourritures terrestres* (1897). Demeter gave the seeds of a pomegranate to her daughter, Persephone.

"Killer Martinis." The host pictured at this outdoor lunch is an old friend, who appears also in "Manhattans," above.

ABOUT THE AUTHOR

CATHARINE SAVAGE BROSMAN, known widely for her poetry, criticism, and essays, is Professor Emerita of French at Tulane University. She is the author of fourteen poetry collections, of which six appeared at LSU Press and five at Mercer University Press. The most recent are *A Memory of Manaus* (2017), *Chained Tree, Chained Owls* (2020), *Clara's Bees* (2021), and *Arm in Arm* (2022). Her poems have appeared widely throughout the United States and also in England and in France, in French translation. She has given scores of readings around the United States and in England. Short fiction of hers was published in 2019 under the title *An Aesthetic Education and Other Stories*; a new and enlarged edition was released in 2022. Her fields of scholarly specialization are French literary history and criticism and, secondarily, American regional literary history and biography. Her studies in the latter field are *Louisiana Creole Literature* (2013), *Southwestern Women Writers and the Vision of Goodness* (2016), *Louisiana Poets: A Literary Guide* (2019), with Olivia McNeely Pass, and *Mississippi Poets: A Literary Guide* (2020). A native of Colorado, she lived nearly forty years in New Orleans before moving to Houston in 2007. She considers her literary home to be Louisiana and now maintains a pied-à-terre in New Orleans.

AVAILABLE FROM GREEN ALTAR BOOKS

If you enjoyed this book, perhaps some of our other titles will pique your interest. The following titles are now available for your reading pleasure... Enjoy!

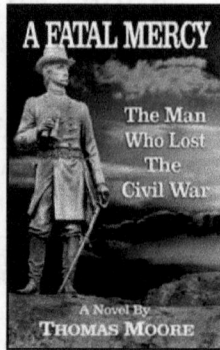

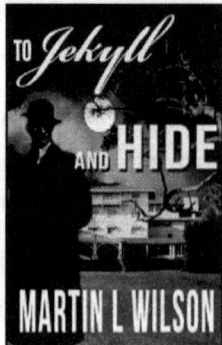

GA

GREEN ALTAR BOOKS
SHOTWELL PUBLISHING